Riches of the Heart

Sixty-Second Readings that Make a Difference

Steve Goodier

First Edition

Life Support System ❤ Publishing, Inc.
P.O. Box 260804 Highlands Ranch, CO 80163-0804
www.LifeSupportSystem.com

Riches of the Heart

Sixty-Second Readings that Make a Difference

By Steve Goodier

Life Support System♡Publishing, Inc.
P.O. Box 260804 Highlands Ranch, CO 80163-0804

Library of Congress Card Number: 99-067867

ISBN 1-929664-01-X (Softcover)

Cover design: Brent Stewart

Contents

Secret Ingredient

When I begin to feel sorry for myself, I sometimes think of Wendy Stoker. In high school, she placed third in the Iowa girl's state diving championships. She practiced for two hours every day for four years to become an accomplished diver.

Then, at the University of Florida, Wendy worked even harder and earned the number two spot on the varsity diving team. At the same time, she carried a full academic load and found time for bowling and water-skiing. But perhaps the most remarkable thing about Wendy Stoker is her typing. Would you believe forty-five words a minute -- with her *toes*? You see, Wendy was born without arms.

Wendy is motivated by a secret ingredient; one of her greatest assets -- desire. With it, one can succeed in spite of overwhelming handicaps. Without it, one is handicapped in spite of overwhelming ability. Desire is a major ingredient in a life which strives to be whole and happy.

A Living Message

Vincent Van Gogh was not always an artist. In fact, he wanted to be a church pastor and was even sent to the Belgian mining community of Borinage in 1879. He discovered that the miners there endured deplorable working conditions and poverty-level wages. Their families were malnourished and struggled simply to survive. He felt concerned that the small stipend he received from the church allowed him a moderate life-style, which, in contrast to the poor, seemed unfair.

One cold February evening, while he watched the miners trudging home, he spotted an old man staggering toward him across the fields, wrapped in a burlap sack for warmth. Van Gogh immediately laid his own clothing out on the bed, set aside enough for one change, and determined to give the rest away. He gave the old man a suit of clothes and he gave his overcoat to a pregnant woman whose husband had been killed in a mining accident. He lived on starvation rations and spent his stipend on food for the miners. When children in one family contracted typhoid fever, though feverish himself, he packed up his bed and took it to them.

A prosperous family in the community offered him free room and board. But Van Gogh declined the offer, stating that it was the final temptation he must reject if he was to faithfully serve his community of poor miners. He believed that if he wanted them to trust him, he must become one of them. And if they were to learn of the love of God through him, he must love them enough to share with them.

He was acutely aware of a wide chasm which can separate words and actions. He knew that people's lives often speak louder and clearer than their words. Maybe it was that same knowledge that led Francis of Assisi to frequently remind his monks, "Wherever you go, preach. Use words if necessary."

Today, others will be "listening" carefully to your actions.

P.S.

Speaking of actions, it has been scientifically proven that the number of people watching you is directly proportional to the stupidity of your action...

So You Have Enemies?

A knight returned to his castle at twilight. He was a mess. His armor was dented, his helmet askew, his face was bloody, his horse was limping and he listed to one side in the saddle. His lord met him at the gate, asking, "What has befallen you, Sir Knight?"

Straightening himself up as best he could, he replied, "Oh, Sire, I have been laboring in your service, robbing and burning and pillaging your enemies to the west."

"You have been what?" cried the startled nobleman. "But I haven't any enemies to the west!"

"Oh!" said the knight. And then, after a pause, "Well, I think you do now."

What about you? Enemies to the west? Or the north, or the south or the east? None of us will calmly sail through our lives in perfect harmony with everyone we meet. And though most conflict can be resolved along the way, and most of our bruised relationships can eventually be healed, some passionate issues may threaten to drive a permanent wedge between people. Heart-felt moral and political stances, especially, can polarize folks who just as passionately hold differing positions.

Former US Ambassador Claire Booth Luce once observed: "I don't have a warm personal enemy left. They've all died off. I miss them terribly because they helped define me."

So-called "enemies" can serve a valuable purpose. If we let them, they can teach us about ourselves. By holding a mirror before us, they can help us see what we may have missed. By disagreeing with our heart-felt convictions, they can sharpen our points of view. And, if we allow it, they can unwittingly help us practice strength and compassion in the face of criticism.

If enemies cannot become friends, they can become teachers. If we listen, they will teach us what our friends cannot.

Thrown from the Bull

Speaker Andy Sherman tells about learning to ride bulls in the rodeo. At eighteen, he told his father he wanted to be a professional bull rider. His father said, "You want to do *what*? Why would you want to do that?"

Andy said jokingly, "I don't know -- I guess I like the hours. You just work eight seconds at a time. That appeals to me."

His father, concerned about the inherent danger, responded, "I absolutely forbid you to do that!" And, at that moment, young Andy instantly knew his life's calling!

The only problem was -- he couldn't ride. Always 7 1/2 seconds away from making the eight second buzzer, he decided to enter "Rodeo School."

The first day of school he was told to get on a bull. He got on and was immediately thrown off. The instructor said, "Get on another one." He was thrown from a second bull. Then a third. And a fourth. He finally asked the instructor, "Are you going to show me how to ride these things?"

"That's how you ride them," came the reply. "Just get on one and ride."

By the week's end, Andy had climbed on, and been thrown off, about eighty bulls. But he learned how to ride.

Experience can be a great teacher. Unfortunately, there is only one way to get it, and that is to fall a few times until you learn. Like the employer who told her new employee, "I hired you to make *right* decisions.

"And how do I do that?" he asked.

"Experience!" she answered.

"How do I get experience?" he asked.

"Wrong decisions."

But experience will never come if we are afraid to try. And fail. And try again. And maybe fail again. We may have to "get thrown from a lot of bulls" if we are ever going to learn to ride. But that is part of living a full and happy life!

P.S.

I suppose that some folks could retire comfortably in their old age if they could sell their experience for what it cost them...

The Power of Forgiveness

During the American Civil War, a young man named Roswell McIntyre was drafted into the New York Cavalry. The war was not going well. Soldiers were needed so desperately, that he was sent into battle with very little training. Roswell became frightened -- he panicked and ran. He was later court-martialed and condemned to be shot for desertion.

McIntyre's mother appealed to President Lincoln. She pleaded that he was young and inexperienced and he needed a second chance. The generals, however, urged the president to enforce discipline. Exceptions, they asserted, would undermine the discipline of an already beleaguered army.

Lincoln thought and prayed. Then he wrote a famous statement. "I have observed," he said, "that it never does a boy much good to shoot him."

He wrote this letter in his own handwriting: "This letter will certify that Roswell McIntyre is to be readmitted into the New York Cavalry. When he serves out his required enlistment, he will be freed of any charges of desertion."

That faded letter, signed by the president, is on display in the Library of Congress. Beside it there is a note which reads, "This letter was taken from the body of Roswell McIntyre, who died at the battle of Little Five Forks, Virginia."

It never does a boy (or anybody else for that matter) much good to shoot him. But you might be surprised at the power of forgiveness.

Choosing Happiness

A customer sat staring sullenly into his drink. "Something wrong?" asked the bartender.

"Well, two months ago," the young man replied, "my grandfather died and left me $85,000 in oil stock."

"That doesn't sound like something to get upset about," said the bartender.

"But last month, my uncle passed away," the young man continued. "He left me $150,000."

"So why are you sitting there so unhappy?"

"Well, this month so far, not a cent!"

Perhaps he had not read Horace's words about how to be happy:

Happy is the man and happy is he alone,
He who can call today his own.
He who is secure within can say,
'Tomorrow do thy worst,
for I have lived today.'"

Today is all we have, really. Now is the best time to choose happiness.

P.S.

Success is getting what you want. Happiness is wanting what you get.

Finding Hope Through Humor

President Ronald Reagan's popularity in the polls rose and fell like a roller-coaster. Shortly after an attempt was made to assassinate him, his ratings soared to nearly 90 percent, the highest on record. But one year later, when the US economy was still mired in recession, his approval ratings had plummeted to a low of 30 percent.

Every other week Dick Wirthlin, the president's pollster, reported the ratings to the president and he now had the unhappy task of telling Reagan the disturbing news.

"How are they? What do the figures look like?" Reagan asked.

"They're pretty bad, Mr. President."

"How bad are they?"

"Well, they're as low as they can get."

"So, what do you mean?"

"Well, they're about 32 percent."

"Anything lower than that in the second year of the presidency?" Reagan asked.

"I think that's the lowest," Wirthlin replied.

Just then Reagan's face brightened and he

smiled, "Dick, Dick, don't worry. I'll just go out there and try to get shot again!"

The president had a knack of effectively bringing humor into his problems which, of course, made them easier to handle. Humor has a way of helping us to find hope. And hope has a way of helping us to solve problems!

Peace

Do not undermine your worth by comparing yourself with others. It is because we are different that each of us is special.

Do not set your goals by what other people deem important. Only you know what is best for you.

Do not take for granted the things closest to your heart. Cling to them as you would your life, for without them, life is meaningless.

Do not let your years slip through your fingers by living in the past, nor in the future. By living your life one day at a time, you live all the days of your life.

Do not give up when you still have something to give. Nothing is really over until the moment you stop trying.

Do not be afraid to encounter risks. It is by taking chances that we learn how to be brave.

Do not shut love out of your life by saying it is impossible to find. The quickest way to receive love is to give love; the fastest way to lose love is to hold it too tightly.

Do not dismiss your dreams. To be without dreams is to be without hope; to be without hope is to be without purpose.

Do not run through life so fast that you forget not only where you have been, but also where you are going. Life is not a race, but a journey to be savored each step of the way.

(Author Unknown)

P.S.

Margaret Bonnano put it well when she said, "It is only possible to live happily ever after on a day to day basis."

God Loves Variety!

I like the story about three ministers and a priest who played golf together every week. They decided to visit each other's churches. So the following day, the three ministers showed up at an early morning mass at their friend's church. There were no empty pews, so they stood in the back.

When the priest saw them, he whispered to the little acolyte, "Get three chairs for the Protestants!" The boy looked stunned and sat down.

The priest pointed in the back to where the clergymen were standing and repeated, "Get three chairs for the Protestants." The confused boy still stared back blankly.

Exasperated, the priest said emphatically, "Please! Get three chairs for the Protestants!"

The dismayed acolyte stood before the congregation and announced, "Ladies and gentlemen. This is the first time this has ever been done in a Catholic church, but let's all stand and give three cheers for the Protestants!"

Perhaps it's time to give three cheers to those of another faith. And while we're at it, let's applaud those of other cultures and races, too! What a beautiful world it is when all are truly part of one glorious family! And after all, if God doesn't love variety, why is there so much of it?

Touch of Wonder

Two little children, a boy and a girl, walked hand-in-hand to their neighbor's house. Standing on her tip-toes, the little girl was just able to reach the doorbell. A woman greeted them and asked what they wanted. "We're playing house," the little girl answered. "This is my husband and I am his wife. May we come in?"

Thoroughly enchanted by the scene confronting her, the lady said, "By all means, do come in."

Once inside, she offered the children lemonade and cookies which they graciously accepted. When a second tall glass of lemonade was offered, the little girl refused by saying: "No thank you. We have to go now. My husband just wet his pants."

Many adults have forgotten what it is like to be a child. They forgot that they once believed the world to be full of magic, wonder and awe. They don't remember to take time for play and have forgotten how to feed their imaginations. For them, ordinary events are now all too commonplace and the extraordinary cannot hold their attention for long. They are not too old to be "awe-struck"!

Does life still hold for you some remnant of magic? Today, you can rekindle that touch of wonder. It's part of being fully alive!

P.S.

Speaking of a child's perspective, one child observed, "Some people can tell the time by looking at the sun, but I have never been able to make out the numbers."

Creating Your Expression

An old story is re-surfacing about a young woman who entered a convent to prepare herself for a life of celibacy and service. The institution was one of a very strict order. Besides other regulations, the convent enforced a requirement of silence -- not a word dare be uttered.

Mother Superior explained to the new recruit that this rule of silence was rigid. However, once every five years just two words could be spoken.

At the end of the first five years of service the young novitiate was called in and instructed that she had earned the privilege of expressing two words. What would they be? Her answer?

"Food rotten!"

Five years later she was again afforded the rare privilege of speaking two more words. What would she say this time?

"Beds hard!"

The third time she was summoned, the woman proclaimed in exasperation, "I quit!"

"Well, good riddance," responded Mother Superior. "All you have ever done since you've been here is to complain!"

It is said that God gives us faces; but we create our own expressions. What expressions will you create today?

We Need Each Other

Many living things need each other to survive. If you have ever seen a Colorado aspen tree, you may have noticed that it does not grow alone. Aspens are found in clusters, or groves. The reason is that the aspen sends up new shoots from the roots. In a small grove, all of the trees may actually be connected by their roots!

Giant California redwood trees may tower 300 feet into the sky. It would seem that they would require extremely deep roots to anchor them against strong winds. But we're told that their roots are actually quite shallow -- in order to capture as much surface water as possible. And they spread in all directions, intertwining with other redwoods. Locked together in this way, all the trees support each other in wind and storms. Like the aspen, they never stand alone. They need one another to survive.

People, too, are connected by a system of roots. We are born to family and learn early to make friends. We are not meant to survive long without others. And like the redwood, we need to hold one another up. When pounded by the sometimes vicious storms of life, we need others to support and sustain us.

Have you been going it alone? Maybe it's time to let someone else help hold you up for awhile. Or perhaps someone needs to hang on to you.

P.S.

If you think cooperation is unnecessary, try to run the automobile on three wheels.

Two Pounds of Enthusiasm

Someone quipped that there is a name for folks who are not excited about their work -- 'unemployed'! People value enthusiasm.

I'm reminded of that great 18th century founder of Methodism, John Wesley. When asked how he drew such large crowds of people to hear him preach, he responded, "I set myself on fire and they come out and watch me burn!" People are drawn to enthusiasm.

Where there is no enthusiasm, there is no passion. Where there is no passion, there is no great living. Are we meant simply to be lukewarm? From antiquity to the present, indifference in any realm has prohibited people from living whole and happy lives.

One woman went to the market and asked for two pounds of sausage. The clerk yelled at the butcher, "Two pounds of enthusiasm!"

"Why do you call it that?" she asked.

"Because he puts everything he's got into it," the clerk said.

In your daily activities, in your various relationships, and in your spiritual pursuits -- what would happen if you "put everything you've got" into it?

What Do You Expect?

Great disappointment can come from unrealistic expectations.

I recently noted that the ex-wife of Robert Lucas, the 1995 winner of the Nobel Memorial Prize in economics, received half of his $1 million award, though they were divorced at the time! As it happens, when they were divorcing in 1988, she had her lawyer add one tiny clause to the property settlement: "Wife shall receive 50 percent of any Nobel prize." More amazing is the fact that her clause had an expiration date: October 31, 1995. He won the prize on October 10. Ironically, Lucas was honored for an economic theory he called, "Rational Expectations."

I admittedly know nothing about Lucas' theory of rational expectations in economics. But I do know something about *irrational* expectations among people. And I know that irrational expectations can cause untold disappointment.

Like the expectation that someone else will make you happy. This is irrational. Nobody can make you happy. That is your job. If you expect it to happen, you will soon be disappointed.

Or the expectation that things should be, for the most part, relatively easy and problem-free. This, too, is irrational. Bad things happen. If you expect things to be easy, you will be in for serious disappointment.

A good question to ask when you are disappointed is, "What did I expect?" Maybe your disappointment is simply the result of irrational expectations.

We can miss out on a lot of happiness because we were expecting something that never could happen. And we can be *in* for a lot of happiness just by changing those unrealistic expectations!

P.S.

Many of us enter marriage clinging to unrealistic expectations. Like George Burns observed: "I was married by a judge. I should have asked for a jury."

Give For the Joy of It!

You may have learned the importance of *saving* money. And you may have learned how to *spend* it wisely. But, have you learned the value of *giving* some of it away? Sharing is an important part of a whole and happy life. And it is a practice that can give back great joy and satisfaction as you make it a part of your regular routine.

I like the story of the chicken and the pig. A chicken and a pig were walking down a street when they spotted a colorful billboard depicting a breakfast plate of eggs and bacon. The chicken stopped to admire the advertisement and said proudly to the pig: "Doesn't that picture make you happy? Doesn't it feel good to be able to give to folks that way?"

The pig replied: "Well, yes, but... for you it's a contribution. For me -- it's total commitment!"

There is a line somewhere between a contribution and commitment. A contribution is made out of obligation, but a voluntary commitment is made out of joy. And when we give out of joy, we feel good!

If you have not yet discovered the value of volunteer giving, try it! You will be pleasantly surprised at how good it can make you feel. And if you wonder about how much you should give away... well, how good do you want to feel?

Joy in the Journey

If you have ever been discouraged because of failure, please read on. For often, achieving what you set out to do is *not* the important thing. Let me explain.

Two brothers decided to dig a deep hole behind their house. As they were working, a couple of older boys stopped by to watch.

"What are you doing?" asked one of the visitors.

"We plan to dig a hole all the way through the earth!" one of the brothers volunteered excitedly.

The older boys began to laugh, telling the younger ones that digging a hole all the way through the earth was impossible. After a long silence, one of the diggers picked up a jar full of spiders, worms and a wide assortment of insects. He removed the lid and showed the wonderful contents to the scoffing visitors. Then he said quietly and confidently, "Even if we don't dig all the way through the earth, look what we found along the way!"

Their goal was far too ambitious, but it did cause them to dig. And that is what a goal is for -- to cause us to move in the direction we have chosen; in other words, to set us to digging!

But not every goal will be fully achieved. Not every job will end successfully. Not every relationship will endure. Not every hope will come to pass. Not every love will last. Not every endeavor will be completed. Not every dream will be realized. But when you fall short of your aim, perhaps you can say, "Yes, but look at what I found along the way! Look at the wonderful things which have come into my life because I tried to do something!"

It is in the digging that life is lived. And I believe it is joy in the journey, in the end, that truly matters.

P.S.

On the other hand, the "philosopher," Yogi Berra, once pointed out, "If you don't know what you're aiming for, you're likely to hit something else!"

Do Something Great

Abraham Lincoln often slipped out of the White House on Wednesday evenings to listen to the sermons of Dr. Phineas Gurley at New York Avenue Presbyterian Church. He generally preferred to come and go unnoticed, so when Dr. Gurley knew the president was coming, he left his study door open. On one of those occasions, the president quietly entered through a side door of the church, took his seat in the minister's study, located just off the sanctuary, and propped the door open just wide enough to hear the preacher.

During the walk home one Wednesday evening, an aide asked Mr. Lincoln his appraisal of the sermon. The president thoughtfully replied, "The content was excellent... he delivered with eloquence... he had put work into the message..."

"Then you thought it was an excellent sermon?" questioned the aide.

"No," Lincoln answered.

"But you said that the content was excellent, it was delivered with eloquence and it showed much work," the aide pressed.

"That's true," Lincoln said. "But Dr. Gurley forgot the most important ingredient. He forgot to ask us to do something great."

There is nothing wrong with average lives and average accomplishments. Most of the good of the world is built on the accumulated efforts of everyday people. But, as Lincoln seemed to know, a life should strive for some greatness.

Are you part of a relationship which, if given more effort, could be outstanding? Do you volunteer for an organization which is truly doing something excellent? Have you joined a cause which is attempting something great? Or have you ever said to yourself concerning a beautiful dream, "I could never do that," while knowing that if you were to attempt it and succeed, you could accomplish something significant?

If Lincoln is right, then every life should strive for some greatness. Including yours and mine!

When Someone Grieves

We either have been, or will be, put in the position of comforting someone who is grieving. That is an important role played by good friends. The most common question I hear on such occasions is, "What should I say?" We want to help, but we feel helpless to make a difference in the face of such tragedy.

I often remember a story told by Joseph Bayly when I struggle to say the "right thing" to someone who is hurting. Mr. Bayly lost three children to death over the course of several years. He wrote a book called, *View From A Hearse*, (Lifejourney Books, 1992) in which he talks about his grief. He says this about comforting those who grieve:

"I was sitting, torn by grief. Someone came and talked to me of God's dealings, of why it happened, of hope beyond the grave. He said things I knew were true. I was unmoved, except to wish he would go away. He finally did. Someone else came and sat beside me. He didn't talk. He didn't ask leading questions. He just sat with me for an hour or more, listened when I said something, answered briefly, prayed simply, left. I was moved. I was comforted. I hated to see him go."

I have found Joseph Bayly's experience to be excruciatingly typical. Both men wanted to help. Both men cared. But only one truly comforted. The difference was that one tried to make him feel better, while the other just let him feel. One tried to say the right things. The other listened. One told him it would be all right. The other shared his pain.

When put in the difficult position of comforting someone in emotional pain, sometimes what needs to be said can be said best with a soft touch or a listening ear. It may not seem like much, but it can be more effective than you may ever know.

P.S.

Speaking of listening, one husband complained, "My wife says I never listen to her. At least I think that's what she said."

The Coach's Way

Bil Keane is the talented artist and humorist who creates the "Family Circus" cartoon. One day, his small son, Jeffy, observed him penciling one of the cartoons. "Daddy," he asked, "how do you know what to draw?"

"God tells me," his father replied.

Then Jeffy said, "Why do you keep erasing parts of it?"

Isn't that the way it is with us? Too often, I find myself with a map in one hand and an eraser in the other. I want to discover and follow the path laid out for me, but I also want to change part of the route at times. Too often, I want to travel an easier path, a more familiar road, or a more comfortable one.

A radio interviewer once said to a player on a championship basketball team: "You are all such talented players. You each have incredible ability. Don't you sometimes want to do your own thing? Isn't it hard for you to do it the coach's way?"

"Oh, no," the player responded. "You see, his way *is* our way."

I am learning that as we journey this path of life, the coach's way *is* our way. We don't have to be afraid to throw away the eraser and trust the map, even when the way seems rough or unfamiliar.

Listen to the coach. It's the way to win!

The Guilt Kit

I read of a New Jersey artist who capitalized on people's needless guilt by selling them "guilt kits." Each kit contained ten disposable brown paper bags and a set of instructions which said, "Place bag securely over your mouth, take a deep breath and blow the guilt out. Dispose of bag immediately." Amazingly, about 2,500 kits sold at $2.50 each! The artist was in tune with just how much guilt people seem to carry around with them.

Of course, guilt serves its purpose, and I understand the use of the kit as a symbol of ridding ourselves of unnecessary, or destructive guilt. But guilt might better be handled at its root. To live free from needless guilt, try these steps:

1. If a mistake was made, resolve never to repeat that mistake. The whole function of guilt is to change behavior.

2. Seek forgiveness from any others who were affected, if possible.

3. Use your spiritual resources. There is great power in knowing that, in an ultimate sense, you are forgiven.

4. Forgive yourself. No purpose is served in continuing to whip yourself over past events you can do nothing else about.

If you follow these steps, you can rid your life of unnecessary guilt. I believe that you will find that you are happier and healthier -- and you can save the brown paper bags for lunch!

P.S.

We put the 'fun' in dysfunctional!

The Touchstone

Do you know the story of the touchstone? It tells of a fortunate man who was told that, if he should possess the "touchstone," its magical powers could give him anything he wanted. The touchstone could be found, he was informed, among the pebbles of a certain beach. All he need do is pick up a stone -- if it feels warm to the touch, unlike the other pebbles, he has found the magical touchstone.

The man went immediately to the beach and began picking up stones. When he grasped a pebble that felt cold, he threw it into the sea. This practice he continued hour after hour, day after day, week after week. Each pebble felt cold. Each pebble was immediately tossed into the sea.

But then, late one morning, he happened to take hold of a pebble which felt warm, unlike the other stones. The man, who's consciousness had barely registered the difference, tossed it into the sea. He hadn't meant to, but he had formed a habit!

Any behavior that we repeat, we reinforce. If we repeat it often enough, it becomes habit. That, of course, can work to our advantage or work against us, depending on the behavior.

Is there a behavior you would like to make into a habit? Then reinforce it by repeating that behavior at every opportunity. Is there a behavior you wish to change? Then substitute another one and repeat the new one often. In this way you build the kind of life you want... day by day.

Prescription For Happiness

Attributed to Robert Louis Stevenson, this prescription for happiness bears remembering and repeating.

*Make up your mind to be happy. Learn to find
pleasure in simple things.*

*Make the best of your circumstances. No one has
everything and everyone has something of sorrow
intermingled with the gladness of life. The trick is to
make the laughter outweigh the tears. Don't take
yourself too seriously.*

*You can't please everybody; don't let criticism
worry you.*

Don't let your neighbor set your standards.

Do the things you enjoy doing, but stay out of debt.

*Don't borrow trouble. Imaginary things are harder
to bear than the actual ones.*

Since hate poisons the soul, do not cherish enmities and grudges.

Don't hold post-mortems. Don't spend your life brooding over sorrows and mistakes. Don't be one who never gets over things.

Do what you can for those less fortunate than yourself.

Keep busy at something. A very busy person never has time to be unhappy.

For maximum effectiveness, this prescription should be taken as often as needed. Unlimited refills available. Share with your friends.

P.S.

Edward Everett Hale advised, "We should never attempt to bear more than one kind of trouble at a time. Some people try to bear three kinds -- all they have had, all they have now, and all they expect to have."

The World Will Come Out All Right

Robert Orben quips that we owe a lot to science. "Thanks to modern medicine," he says, "we are no longer forced to endure prolonged pain, disease, discomfort and wealth."

Medical treatment is expensive, but most of us will pay what we can to stay healthy. We realize, too, that good health also includes a healthy mind and spirit. Whole and healthy people are happy people. And healthy people make for a healthy world.

A psychiatrist tore a picture of the world from a magazine and cut it into tiny pieces. "Take these puzzle pieces," he said to a young boy, "and put the world back together."

In just a few moments the smiling child returned with the completed picture. "How did you do it so quickly?" the amazed doctor asked.

"Easy!" said the boy. "I noticed that there is a picture of a man on the other side. I just put the man together and the world came out all right."

If each of us becomes whole -- body, mind, and spirit -- won't the world come out all right?

Heroes Among Us

Not every Marine is a hero! During field training exercises at Parris Island, South Carolina, one drill instructor threw a pine cone among the recruits and yelled, "Grenade!" The trainees immediately turned away and hit the ground. "Just as I suspected," chided the DI. "Not a hero among you! Didn't anyone want to jump on that grenade to save the others?"

A little later the instructor threw another pine cone and yelled, "Grenade!" This time, all the recruits but one jumped on the "explosive."

"Why are you still standing there?" the DI demanded.

"Sir," the recruit replied, "someone had to live to tell about it."

Not everyone is a hero. But then, not every hero is instantly recognizable. For heroes do not always wear uniforms and perform mighty acts of valor.

Do you know a hero? I think perhaps you do. Heroes, you see, can be found in some of the most unexpected places! I knew a young mother who was slowly dying of cancer from a hospital bed, yet she put aside her pain long enough every day to smile and laugh with her children. And I watched her husband fill the roles of single parent and financial provider, and still spend every remaining moment sitting at his mate's bedside, valiantly encouraging and offering whatever hope he could muster.

I have known talented teachers who could have worked at far more lucrative professions, yet were determined to stay in a disadvantaged school in the hope that some of their kids might succeed.

I have known students who, against great obstacles at home, persevered in the hope of someday "making something" of themselves.

I have known people from all walks of life face their difficulties with optimism, determination and courage, daily overcoming the impossible. These are the heroes among us.

Many of the world's true heroes have never seen battle, cannot compete athletically and will never sing in a pop band. They have been too busy plodding away in less glorified arenas.

Do you know a hero? Perhaps one lives in your home. And quite likely, one looks back at you from the mirror. For it is in these everyday battles of the spirit that true wars are fought and won. And it is these "everyday" heroes who remind us that anything is possible, one day at a time.

P.S.

Some people just don't get it! One person prayed, "Grant me strength to change the things I can, grace to accept the things I cannot change, and a great big bag of money."

Your Heart's Music

It was 1994. Daily, the city of Sarajevo was under siege. Mortars and artillery fire instantly transformed once beautiful buildings into rubble. Sarajevo's citizens were frightened, weary and increasingly despondent. Then, one February day, a mortar shell exploded in the market killing 68 civilians. Many more were wounded and maimed from the blast.

A cellist with the Sarajevo symphony could no longer stand the killing. He took his cello to the market, sat down amidst the rubble and played a concert. When he finished, he simply took up his instrument and left.

Every day, for 67 days, he came to the market. Every day he played a concert. It was his gift of love to the city. He did it because he felt his community needed hope.

Hope is music in the heart. It is a gift given to each of us to see us through the night. Once you have lost hope, you have nothing left to lose. Utter hopelessness kills everything it touches. But hope gives us strength to continue, whether it be a marriage that is worth saving, a life that is worth living or a situation that is worth salvaging.

In the end, hope is a spiritual thing. When all is in chaos and ruin, hope is the knowledge that the music still goes on. In this vast and infinite universe, we are not alone.

During those times when all may seem to be crumbling down around you, can you hear the music in your heart -- the song of hope? Listen carefully. It is there, playing for you.

Serious Humor

I heard of a mortuary director with a sense of humor. He signs all his correspondence: "Eventually Yours."

Laughter is a wonderful coping devise. It helps us to successfully traverse dangerous currents along life's journey, as well as assisting us to fully enjoy the placid times of still waters. Humor is something I can get serious about. It is nothing less than an extravagant gift -- to be frequently used and shared! I believe it was Billy Graham who said that "a keen sense of humor helps us to overlook the unbecoming, understand the unconventional, tolerate the unpleasant, overcome the unexpected, and outlast the unbearable."

The best part of all is that you have already received the gift of laughter! Will you use it and share it often today?

P.S.

It is well said: "Who laughs last, laughs best, the wise-acres vow; but I am impatient, I want to laugh now!"

Listening With Your Answer Running

There is a story out of Edinburg, Scotland, about a woman who was resolutely opposed to street-corner evangelism. One Sunday evening she was waiting for a streetcar at the Mound, a location used by various orators, and on that day by a well-known evangelist.

The meeting had just finished when, to her horror, she saw the evangelist heading straight for her. She gathered her strength and had her answer ready. So when the poor man politely said, "Excuse me, Madam, but does the number six car go to Marchmont?" she snapped back, "That's a matter between *me* and *my God*!"

She answered a question that was never asked. She had not heard the man because she was "listening with her answer running."

A sure way for wives and husbands, parents and children, employers and employees, people of all acquaintances to misunderstand one another is to listen with their answers running.

Today, give your *whole* attention to others and discover what a difference it makes!

First Things First

A young ensign had nearly completed his first overseas tour of duty when he was given the opportunity to prepare his ship to "set sail." With a stream of crisp commands, he had the decks buzzing with sailors and soon the ship was churning slowly out of the channel.

The ensign's efficiency was remarkable. In fact, the talk was that he had set a new record for getting the ship underway. His bubble was burst, however, when he was handed a radio message from the captain.

"My personal congratulations upon completing your underway preparation exercise according to the book and with amazing speed," it read. "But next time wait until your captain is aboard before getting underway!"

What good is a ship without the captain? The ensign did all the right things, but he never did the most important thing!

It is a matter of priorities. You may accomplish a great deal every day. But are you accomplishing the truly important things? To borrow the language of Stephen Covey, have you put first things first?

In marriage and relationships, in work and career, in the areas of mental, physical and spiritual health, are you truly doing the important things?

It is never a matter of doing *more*. To determine to squeeze more time in every day for exercise, reading or spiritual devotion usually does not last long. More people find success in deciding what is truly important and doing it first. And if some of the other "stuff" never gets done, will you miss it?

Today, will you put first things first? And how about tomorrow? And the next day? If so, you will one day discover that you are building a life that counts.

P.S.

Twenty years from now you will be more disappointed by the things that you didn't do than by the ones you did do. So throw off the bowlines. Sail away from the safe harbor. Catch the trade winds in your sails. Explore. Dream. Discover ~ *Mark Twain*

Growing Good Corn

James Bender, in his book *How to Talk Well* (New York: McGraw-Hill Book Co., Inc., 1994) relates the story of a farmer who grew award-winning corn. Each year he entered his corn in the state fair where it won a blue ribbon.

One year a newspaper reporter interviewed him and learned something interesting about how he grew it. The reporter discovered that the farmer shared his seed corn with his neighbors.

"How can you afford to share your best seed corn with your neighbors when they are entering corn in competition with yours each year?" the reporter asked.

"Why sir," said the farmer, "didn't you know? The wind picks up pollen from the ripening corn and swirls it from field to field. If my neighbors grow inferior corn, cross-pollination will steadily degrade the quality of my corn. If I am to grow good corn, I must help my neighbors grow good corn."

He is very much aware of the connectedness of life. His corn cannot improve unless his neighbor's corn also improves.

So it is with our lives. Those who choose to live in peace must help their neighbors to live in peace. Those who choose to live well must help others to live well, for the value of a life is measured by the lives it touches. And those who choose to be happy must help others to find happiness, for the welfare of each is bound up with the welfare of all.

The lesson for each of us is this: if we are to grow good corn, we must help our neighbors grow good corn.

Needless Worry

A story worth dusting off is about a man who bragged: "I only worry about two things -- whether I am sick or well. If I'm well, I have nothing to worry about! And if I'm sick, I've only got two things to worry about -- whether I get better, or whether I die. If I get better, I have nothing to worry about! And if I die, I've only got two things to worry about -- whether I go to heaven or hell. If I go to heaven, I have nothing to worry about. And if I go to hell, I'll be so busy greeting my friends I won't have time to worry! So why worry?"

Regardless of how you feel about his view of life after life, he makes a good point about worry! There is really no room for needless concern about the future. I like what Ralph Waldo Emerson said about worry:

Some of your hurts you have cured,
And the sharpest you still have survived,
But what torments of grief you endured
From evil that never arrived!

Almost without our being aware, healthy concern can be transformed into cancerous worry. And though it is true that most people worry needlessly at times, many of us feel consumed with worry too much of the time. We find ourselves "enduring torments of grief" from evils that have not yet arrived and probably never will.

What needless worries can you release today?

P.S.

Herm Albright has a different take on attitude. He says, "A positive attitude will not solve all your problems, but it will annoy enough people to make it worth the effort..."

Just Do What You Know!

News commentator Paul Harvey (February 9, 1981) related a story which took place during the Carter administration. Evidently, daughter Amy Carter needed help with some homework. It was Friday and the assignment, a question about the Industrial Revolution, was due on Monday. Neither Amy nor her mother quite understood the question, so mother Rosalyn asked a White House aide to run the question by the Labor Department.

Sunday afternoon a truck pulled up at the White House loaded with a computer printout. Someone assumed the president needed the information urgently, so the Labor Department assigned a team to work all weekend to prepare the documents.

When Rosalyn learned that the research had cost hundreds of thousands of taxpayer dollars she was horrified! But Amy went ahead and used the information to complete her homework.

On that homework assignment, by the way, Amy got a "C". (Does that say something about the quality of information they gathered?)

I see a parable here. You and I also possess a "truckload" of information. We have spent a lifetime gathering data about even the smallest aspects of our lives. But, in the end, it's what we *do* with all of that information that matters.

My own life can improve significantly if I simply take what I already know and *apply* it. I know how to forgive, for example, yet I am slow to do it. I know how to love, when to be patient and how to share generously. But I don't always *do* these things.

Most of the time I even know how to be happy. I bet that you do, too. And I also know that if I habitually *do* those things which I know will bring happiness, I will not be disappointed.

I believe most of us know what to do; we simply have *to do what we know!* A full and happy life does not result from merely getting more information. It is a product of daily application!

In the Cement Mixer

Did you ever have a day like this? A man, cleaning one of those big cement trucks, got caught in the mixer. He climbed into the mixer with a hose to flush out the remaining cement when his hose caught on a lever and pulled it to the "on" position. Suddenly, he found himself going round and round in the mixer with no way to escape! Slipping, sliding and banging around inside, all he could do was shout for help.

Fortunately, another worker came over and shut it off. In moments, a bruised and battered man, covered with wet concrete, emerged from the mixer. It reminds me of some days I've had...

Of course, no one ever said life is easy! But, as that incredible humanitarian novelist, Harriet Beecher Stowe, said, "When you get in a tight place and everything goes against you, until it seems as if you could not hold on a minute longer, never give up then, for that is just the place and time when the tide will turn."

If it feels as if you are in the cement mixer, do you need to hold on a little longer?

P.S.

Some people have it rougher than others. Jerry Lewis says, "When I was a kid I said to my father one afternoon, 'Daddy, will you take me to the zoo?' He answered, 'If the zoo wants you, let them come and get you.'"

Choose It!

Two men fell on hard times. Try as they might, they couldn't find work. They heard that a museum was willing to pay $50 apiece for live rattlesnakes so, in desperation, they decided to catch snakes.

Outfitted with a net and basket, they hiked to a remote area renowned for its large snake population. But as they scaled a steep ledge, the rock gave way and they tumbled down the slippery bank -- into a deep pit crawling with rattlesnakes!

One of the men quickly sized up the situation and shouted excitedly to his friend, "Look! We're rich! We're *rich!*"

Some people see good in anything! And I suppose there's usually a brighter side. Take aging, for instance. As we grow older, our skin turns from satin to cotton to seersucker to corduroy. But, on a brighter side, I'm just glad wrinkles don't hurt!

It has to do with how we look at our situation. Like a sign spotted outside a New England shop: "We buy junk. Antiques for sale." Is your attic full of junk or antiques? It's a matter of perspective.

Your greatest power may well be your power to choose. As Abraham Lincoln wisely said, "Most people are about as happy as they make up their minds to be." The truth is, we can *choose* to view many of our problems as opportunities, we can *choose* to age in body without aging in spirit, and we can *choose* to be encouraged by the good of life, rather than discouraged by the bad.

It's your point of view! Choose it!

What Would You Die For?

Do you know what you would die for? An ancient story tells of two great warriors, Cyrus and Cagular. Cyrus, of course, was the noted emperor of Persia and Cagular was a little-known chieftain who consistently repelled Cyrus' attacks.

Cagular's troops tore the Persian army apart time and time again as they resisted Cyrus' attempts to expand his southern border. Finally, Cyrus amassed his whole army, surrounded Cagular, captured him, and brought him to the capitol for trial and execution.

On the day of the trial, Cagular and his family were brought to the judgment chamber. The chieftain, six feet tall with the appearance of a nobleman, faced the throne. Cyrus was duly impressed with Cagular.

"What would you do should I spare your life?" the emperor asked.

"Your majesty," replied the warrior, "If you spared my life, I would return home and remain your obedient servant as long as I live."

"What would you do if I spared the life of your wife?" Cyrus questioned.

"Your majesty, if you spared the life of my wife, I would die for you."

So moved was Cyrus by his answer that he freed Cagular and his wife and appointed the chieftain to govern the southern province.

On the trip home, Cagular enthused to his wife, "Did you notice the marble entrance to the palace? Did you see the corridor to the throne room? Did you see the chair on which he sat? It was made of one lump of solid gold!"

His wife appreciated her husband's excitement, but admitted, "I really didn't notice any of that."

"Well," Cagular asked in amazement, "What did you see?"

She looked seriously into his eyes. "I beheld only the face of the man who said he would die for me."

Do you know what you would die for? Loved ones? Home? Country? Faith? Liberty? Love? Determine what you will die for, and you will have identified what you should *live* for.

Live for the few things you'd *die* for and you will be fully alive! You will also have learned something about how to be happy.

P.S.

Here's some advice from eight-year-old Erin on making love endure: "Don't forget your wife's name... that will mess up the love."

No Problem!

Don't worry if you have problems! Which is easy to say until you are in the midst of a really big one, I know. But the only people I am aware of who don't have troubles are gathered in little neighborhoods. Most communities have at least one. We call them cemeteries.

If you're breathing, you have difficulties. It's the way of life. And believe it or not, most of your problems may actually be good for you! Let me explain.

Maybe you have seen the Great Barrier Reef, stretching some 1,800 miles from New Guinea to Australia. Tour guides regularly take visitors to view the reef. On one tour, the guide was asked an interesting question. "I notice that the lagoon side of the reef looks pale and lifeless, while the ocean side is vibrant and colorful," a traveler observed. "Why is this?"

The guide gave an interesting answer: "The coral around the lagoon side is in still water, with no challenge for its survival. It dies early. The coral on the ocean side is constantly being tested by wind, waves, storms -- surges of power. It has to fight for survival every day of its life. As it is challenged and tested it changes and adapts. It grows healthy. It grows strong. And it reproduces." Then he added this telling note: "That's the way it is with every living organism."

That's how it is with people. Challenged and tested, we come alive! Like coral pounded by the sea, we grow. Physical demands can cause us to grow stronger. Mental and emotional stress can produce tough-mindedness and resiliency. Spiritual testing can produce strength of character and faithfulness.

So, you have problems -- no problem! Just tell yourself, "There I grow again!"

The Last Day

Her husband came back to life! Well, almost... Herlinda Estrada, from Baytown, Texas, was called to the hospital to identify the body of her husband. Jose had gone for a jog that day. But coincidentally, another jogger along the same trail collapsed and died of a heart attack. The victim was taken to the nearby hospital where authorities found a car key in his pocket, but no identification. They took the key back to a parking lot near the jogging trail and tried it in the doors of General Motors cars until they found a fit -- coincidentally, in Jose Estrada's truck! (It wasn't until later that they tested the key in the car of the deceased jogger.) After checking the truck's registration they called Jose's wife and asked her to come to the hospital to positively identify her husband.

The jogger's body was covered by a sheet, a tube snaked from his mouth and his eyes were taped shut. In her distraught condition, Herlinda assumed the body was that of her husband. Even the clothes he had worn looked like Jose's. She signed the death certificate and joined other grieving members of her family in a hospital waiting room.

Meanwhile, Jose, alive and well, finished his jog and drove home. He received a call from a friend who, when she heard his voice, exclaimed, "Jose! You're not dead! They said you were dead!"

He raced to the hospital and, to the astonishment of his grieving family, strode into the waiting room! Herlinda clung to him and laughed and cried, all at the same time. After a while she said, "Jose, if you ever die on me again, I'll kill you myself."

She was never so grateful for her husband until she thought she had lost him. I can't help but think what life might be like if every day were lived in the awesome awareness that the people we love are temporary gifts. Would we feel grateful just to be close to them?

Try living today as if this were your last day with those you love. It just may be... overwhelming! And worth doing again!

Believing In You

Did you know that Albert Einstein could not speak until he was four years old, and did not read until he was seven? His parents and teachers worried about his mental ability.

Beethoven's music teacher said about him, "As a composer he is hopeless." What if young Ludwig believed it?

When Thomas Edison was a young boy, his teachers said he was so stupid he could never learn anything. He once said, "I remember I used to never be able to get along at school. I was always at the foot of my class... my father thought I was stupid, and I almost decided that I was a dunce." What if young Thomas believed what they said about him?

When F. W. Woolworth was 21, he got a job in a store, but was not allowed to wait on customers because he "didn't have enough sense."

When the sculptor Auguste Rodin was young he had difficulty learning to read and write. Today, we may say he had a learning disability, but his father said of him, "I have an idiot for a son."

He uncle agreed. "He's uneducable," he said. What if Rodin had doubted his ability?

Walt Disney was once fired by a newspaper editor because he was thought to have no "good ideas." Caruso was told by one music teacher, "You can't sing. You have no voice at all." And an editor told Louisa May Alcott that she was incapable of writing anything that would have popular appeal.

What if these people had listened and become discouraged? Where would our world be without the music of Beethoven, the art of Rodin or the ideas of Albert Einstein and Thomas Edison? As Oscar Levant has accurately said, "It's not what you are, it's what you don't become that hurts."

You have great potential. When you believe in all you can be, rather than all you cannot become, you will find your place on earth.

P.S.

Of course, nothing is impossible for those who don't have to do it...

No Time to Judge

Eugene Brice, in *Books That Bring Life* (Lubbock, Texas: Net Press 1987), tells of a controversy that consumed the United States Senate many years ago. It was around whether or not to seat the newly elected senator from Utah, Reed Smoot.

Back in those days, the Mormon church (to which Smoot belonged) still allowed the practice of polygamy. And although Smoot had only one wife, some of the more sanctimonious members of the Senate argued that he should not be seated, given the beliefs of his church.

But the issue was settled when Senator Boise Penrose of Pennsylvania strode to the podium and looked directly at some of his colleagues who, though married, were known to "womanize." He stated emphatically, "As for me, I would prefer to have seated beside me in the Senate a polygamist who doesn't polyg than a monogamist who doesn't monog." End of matter.

I think Mother Teresa got it right: "If you judge people, you have no time to love them." And if you love people, you have no desire to judge them.

Besides, there may come a time when we, too, will find ourselves more in need of love than judgement.

Creating An Opportunity

A little boy wanted a taste of molasses from the large barrel by the door of an old-fashioned country store. He slid a box beside the barrel, stepped up on it and leaned over the rim as far as possible, stretching out his finger toward the sweet goo below. He stretched and strained and toppled head first into the barrel.

Dripping with molasses, he stood up, lifted his eyes heaven-ward and was heard to utter, "Lord, help me to make the most of this fantastic opportunity!"

A quality that some people possess is the ability to take whatever life gives them and turn it into an opportunity. David Boren must be such a man. The Oklahoma politician learned from professional pollsters that he would most likely lose his gubernatorial bid, and lose it big. The professional polling agency he hired reported his strength to be about two percent of the population.

His first reaction was to quit. But he finally decided to turn his bad news into an opportunity. He told his listeners, "I had a professional poll taken and it shows I've got great potential for increasing my support!"

That sounded a whole lot better than it was! But he eventually won the election and served as governor of the state of Oklahoma.

Will you accept the creative challenge to take what life gives you and turn it into an opportunity? If so, watch out! Something exciting just might happen!

P.S.

Columnist Anne Landers tells us that "Opportunities are usually disguised as hard work, so most people don't recognize them."

A Healthy Dose of Laughter

I read that a child laughs 400 times a day on the average, while an adult laughs only 15 times each day. Which is puzzling since laughter feels so good and is so good for us!

You may know the benefits of laughter on the mind and spirit, but are you aware of how much a good laugh can help you physically? Norman Cousins used to say that laughter is so beneficial for your body that it is like "inner jogging."

Mayo Clinic (*Mayo Clinic Health Letter*, March 1993) reports that laughter aids breathing by disrupting your normal respiration pattern and increasing your breathing rate. It can even help clear mucus from your lungs.

Laughter is also good for your heart. It increases circulation and improves the delivery of oxygen and nutrients to tissues throughout your body.

A good laugh helps your immune system fight off colds, flu and sinus problems by increasing the concentration of immunoglobulin A in your saliva. And it may help control pain by raising the levels of certain brain chemicals (endorphins).

Furthermore, it is a natural stress reliever. Have you ever laughed so hard that you doubled over, fell off your chair, spit out your food or wet your pants? You cannot maintain muscle tension when you are laughing!

The good news is that you are allowed more than 15 laughs a day! Go ahead and double the dose and make it 30 times today. (You may begin to notice immediate improvement in your relationships!) Then double it again! You are bound to feel better, you will cope with problems more effectively and people will enjoy being around you.

Laughter: it's just good medicine!

Perpetual Learning

I recently read of a study of ninety top leaders in a variety of fields. Interviewers were trying to determine just what it is that sets leaders apart. They discovered that those who rise to the top of their professions have the never-ending capacity to develop and improve their skills. In other words, leaders are perpetual learners.

But shouldn't we always walk that path of learning? When do we feel as if we now know enough? When should personal growth end?

I once visited a friend who had just celebrated her 80th birthday. Jessie talked with much enthusiasm about a quilt she had recently finished making for her great-grandson. She wanted the center square to be special and asked him what picture he would like for that square. The little boy replied, "I want a turtle."

Jessie had never made a turtle. "How about a dog?" she suggested. "Or a house? I can't make a turtle."

"Well, Gramma," he said. "I think you're old enough to learn."

And she did! The finished quilt had a turtle right in the middle!

Jessie was especially proud of that quilt because she learned to do something new. And she discovered that he was right -- she *was* old enough to learn!

Are you a perpetual learner? It's part of building a whole and happy life.

P.S.

One man said that he asked his wife, "Will you love me when I'm old and senile?" She said, "Of course, I do."

One Light

Imagine an artist painting a winter scene. She depicts a white, frozen ground and evergreens draped in snow. Her hand brings the day to a close as she paints night falling on the canvas. In the deep shadows of dusk, she has painted a grim, log cabin, barely visible to the casual observer.

Then she dips her brush in yellow paint and, with a few quick strokes, places a brightly burning lamp in one of the cabin's windows. Warm rays dance on white snow, now made brighter by the light. The lonely lamp wholly changes the tone of the picture, replacing feelings of dark and gloom with warmth and security.

Edith Wharton has said that there are two ways of spreading the light: to be the candle or the mirror that reflects it. Sometimes we are candles. We shed light of love and hope. We shine encouragement into dark souls. Or we illuminate with insight.

But sometimes we reflect the light. We are mirrors to enable others to see the light of their own goodness and beauty. And when we have no other light of our own, we are mirrors which reflect a greater Light.

For some, the world can be bleak and cold. They feel frightened, lonely and even hopeless. But it's true that no amount of darkness can extinguish the light of one, small candle. You?

Living Fully

Do you feel your life is all it can be? Do you yearn for life to be fuller? A friend once recited this poem to me:

There once was a cautious gal,
who never romped or played;
She never drank, she never smoked,
from the path she never strayed.
So when she passed away
the insurance was denied;
For since she never really lived
they claimed she never died!

Of course, I don't think these behaviors describe quality living, but I do think most people want to experience life as fully as possible. This has always been the case. Even two thousand years ago, Jesus, that great lover of life from Galilee, recognized our universal yearning for *life* when he said, "I have come that they might have life and have it more abundantly."

And, of course, "romping," "playing," and "straying from the path" have little to do with how fully one experiences life. Abundant living is more about how we love the other people on this planet, how we care for ourselves and how well we honor our God. It has to do with joy and laughter, kindness, forgiveness and peace. It means taking time for what is truly necessary.

One man was asked if he believed in life after death. His wife spoke first. "Life after death?" she said. "He doesn't even believe in life after dinner!"

I believe in life after death. But I also believe in life *before* death. Abundant and full and beginning today.

P.S.

Dr. Elizabeth Kubler-Ross said this about light: "People are like stained-glass windows. They sparkle and shine when the sun is out, but when the darkness sets in, their true beauty is revealed only if there is a light from within."

Legacy of Love

A friend once told me of a caring and much-loved school nurse who died. She was well-known by the faculty and students as she had been there 35 years. When the principal announced her death to the children, many of them began to cry.

To help ease their grief, the school counselor had a group of children draw a picture of what the nurse meant to them. One child filled in her paper with red. "This is her heart," she explained. "It's too big for the paper."

At her funeral her friends and family clapped and celebrated her life. She left behind a great legacy of love.

How will you be remembered? What legacy will you leave behind?

Toward the end of his life, Elton Trueblood made this observation. "At the age of 93, I am well aware that I do not have many years to live. Consequently, I try very hard to live my remaining years in such a manner that I really make a difference in as many lives as possible. How do I want to be remembered? Not primarily as a Christian scholar, but rather as a loving person. This can be the goal of every individual. If I can be remembered as a truly loving person, I shall be satisfied."

After you are gone, people may forget most of what you have done. But they will remember whether you loved them.

Shuffling Priorities

It happened on the evening of April 14, 1912. The Titanic, the largest ship afloat, struck an iceberg in the treacherous waters of the Atlantic. Four hours later she sank to the bottom.

A place on one lifeboat was reserved for a certain woman. She was just stepping into the boat when she asked if she could run to the ship's library to get something. She was allowed three minutes.

The woman ran through the corridors of the reeling vessel. Crossing the saloon she caught sight of jewelry strewn around the floor. Passengers had hurriedly cleaned out their safes and dropped valuables as they ran. What an opportunity! Wealth was literally at her fingertips!

But she ignored the jewelry, made her way to the library, snatched a copy of the Bible and ran back to the waiting lifeboat.

Earlier that day it may have seemed incredible to the woman to choose a copy of the Bible over valuable jewelry. But in the face of death, prized valuables became relatively worthless, and what may have seemed worthless became suddenly valuable.

Unfortunately, it often takes a catastrophe to shuffle our priorities into a sensible order. But what a catastrophe when we never do discover what is truly valuable.

P.S.

Don't just count your blessings, make your blessings count!

Act As If

What final result are you trying to achieve?

In the mid-1950s, a flamboyant, but unknown, American pianist had dreams of performing in the Hollywood Bowl. He gathered some money, rented the Hollywood Bowl on an off night, showed up wearing a tuxedo and played a full concert on a grand piano to absolutely no audience at all.

Except that the hall was empty, he lived his dream. Then he kept building on that dream until, four years later to the very night, Liberace performed at the Hollywood Bowl before a capacity, standing-room-only crowd.

Several years prior, it was Harry Emerson Fosdick who voiced a new thought about self transformation. He said, "Hold a picture of yourself long and steadily enough in your mind's eye and you will be drawn toward it. Picture yourself vividly as defeated and that alone will make victory impossible. Picture yourself vividly as winning and that alone will contribute immeasurably to success. Great living starts with a picture, held in your imagination of what you would like to do or be."

Liberace had one major goal at first -- the Hollywood Bowl. He held that picture in his mind, then acted as if he had already achieved it, and it came to pass. These are two necessary steps to achieving any result, regardless how big or small: hold a picture of the dream in your mind and act as if it were already so.

It is especially true in the area of self-transformation. Whether you want to overcome shyness, kick a habit, find a fulfilling relationship or achieve a long-held dream, the process is the same. Picture it in your mind then act as if you were already self-confident, as if you were already free from the habit, or as if you were perfectly capable of growing that relationship. Don't be surprised if the results are remarkable!

The Pilot Smiled

You might be tossing about in a sea of despair. You might even feel as if your life may crash about you and you will never again be healed, whole or happy.

They say Robert Louis Stevenson told the story first. It's worth retelling: It seems a storm caught a sea-faring vessel off a rocky coast. The wind and waves threatened to drive the boat to its destruction.

In the midst of the terror, one daring passenger, contrary to orders, made his way across the ship. Groping along a passageway, he found the pilot house. There he beheld an intriguing sight; the ship's pilot was lashed to his post. Secure against the raging elements, he held the wheel fast, turning the ship, inch by inch, once more out to sea. The pilot saw the watcher and smiled.

The daring passenger found his way below deck where other passengers huddled. Encouragingly, he said, "I have seen the face of the pilot, and he smiled. All is well."

There are times we need to hear that. Especially when we feel tossed about by a raging storm, it helps to remember that the pilot smiles.

Can you imagine the pilot smiling now?

P.S.

Speaking of being tossed about at sea... a London newspaper reported: "A young girl, who was blown out to sea on a set of inflatable teeth, was rescued by a man on an inflatable lobster. A coast-guard spokesman commented, 'This sort of thing is all too common these days...'"

Learn To Love Them!

Are you ever frustrated with people you care about? Are you *more* frustrated because it seems as if they just won't change?

A man tried everything he could think of to eradicate the weeds in his lawn. Finally, in desperation, he wrote to the Department of Agriculture asking advice, and listing every method he had tried.

He received a reply back. It said, "We suggest you learn to love them!"

The same could be said about marriage and friendship. We may feel exasperated by the faults and idiosyncrasies of others. We believe the relationship would be perfect if only they would change that annoying habit or correct that irritating behavior.

So we embark on a campaign to "get rid of the weeds" -- to get someone we care about to change. We may nag and cajole and plead and bribe. And in the end, we feel frustrated because they are still the same!

The truth is, we cannot, and should not, attempt to eradicate the "weeds" we find in other's lives. We can never change others. They *can* change, but *we* can't change them. The will to change must come from within themselves. Rather, our task is simply to learn to love them, weeds and all.

Isn't this the way we want them to treat us? And besides, like a lovely garden, they become more attractive to us when we are not focussed on the weeds. We might even begin to enjoy them so much that we remember what drew us to them in the first place!

Listen Louder

A man realized he needed to purchase a hearing aid, but he felt unwilling to spend much money. "How much do they run?" he asked the clerk.

"That depends," said the salesman. "They run from $2.00 to $2,000."

"Let's see the $2.00 model," he said.

The clerk put the device around the man's neck. "You just stick this button in your ear and run this little string down to your pocket," he instructed.

"How does it work?" the customer asked.

"For $2.00 -- it doesn't work," the salesman replied. "But when people see it on you, they'll talk louder!"

As you know, most communication problems are not due to people talking too softly. Unfortunately, we are not always good listeners. Do you know that people will pay hundreds of dollars an hour for no other reason than to have someone listen to them?

Psychologist Carl Rogers said, "A person's real need, a most terrible need, is for someone to listen. . . not as a 'patient' but as a human soul." To listen well is to respond to a great human yearning.

One small child put it like this: "I'll try to listen louder." What might happen if you "listened louder" today?

P.S.

It was Pythagoras who said, "Learn to be silent. Let your quiet mind listen and absorb." Was listening also a problem way back then?

Love Letter to a Cat

A love letter to a cat? Why not? At least Andrew thought it might work. This is an actual love letter written by a boy to his cat.

But before you read the letter, you must understand this about the cat. She is about as affectionate as a cactus. And besides, she goes to great lengths to avoid Andrew. She would rather sleep the day away in one of her many hiding places scattered throughout the boy's house than be near him. And on one of those rare occasions when she makes an appearance, he can forget about touching her. If he never has anything to do with her, that is all right by the cat.

The boy tries his best to be nice. He looks for her, searching the house for an occupied hiding place, and feels abundantly grateful if he should stumble upon his treasure. He is occasionally allowed to stroke her once or twice before she flits off. He even feeds her, hoping to eventually win her confidence and perhaps even a bit of affection. But he is seldom rewarded with anything like attention.

Now that you know something about the cat,

whose name is Mehitabel, by the way, what about the love letter? It was found next to the cat's food dish. This is what it said: "To cat (he couldn't spell Mehitabel!): I love you. Before you love me I will love you more. Love, Andrew. Meow!"

What a selfless love! "I love you. Before you love me I will love you more." That is the kind of patient love a parent may have for a child. And the kind of love God has for us, God's children.

There is something beautifully excessive about a love which says, "Before you love me I will love you more." I believe we can use more excessive lovers!

Filling Up Your Life

We can live a long time without thinking about such things as "meaning" and "purpose" in life. But happy and healthy living requires that we visit these words from time to time

I have heard that Ralph Barton, a cartoonist of a former generation, left this note pinned to his pillow before taking his life: "I have had few difficulties, many friends, great successes; I have gone from wife to wife, and from house to house, visited great countries of the world, but I am fed up with inventing devices to fill up twenty-four hours of the day."

Whatever psychological problems may have afflicted him, Ralph Barton suffered from an empty life. He tried to fill it up -- with relationships and things and busyness. He was no doubt successful in his work. And probably well-liked. His problem was that he felt his life had no meaning.

Educator Morrie Schwartz helps us put meaning into our lives. In Mitch Albom's audiobook, *Tuesdays with Morrie* (Grand Haven, MI: Nova Audio Books, Brilliance, 1997), he chronicles the final months of Morrie's life, as his former teacher slowly dies of Lou Gehrig's Disease (ALS). Morrie, that irrepressible lover of life, says this: "So many people walk around with a meaningless life. They seem half asleep even when they are busy doing things they think are important. This is the product of chasing the wrong things. The way you get meaning into your life is to devote yourself to loving others, to devote yourself to your community around you, and devote yourself to creating something that gives you purpose and meaning."

Do you want to be happy? Do you want a life that matters? Then fill it up with loving and caring for those around you! I guarantee, it will never seem empty again!

P.S.

Speaking of leading a meaningful life, Ashleigh Brilliant quipped: "Life may have no meaning. Or even worse, it may have a meaning of which I disapprove."

Three Powerful Words

A funny story is told about General George Patton from his World War II days. He once accepted an invitation to dine at a press camp in Africa. Wine was served in canteen cups but, obviously thinking he was served coffee, Patton poured cream into his cup. As he stirred in sugar, Patton was warned that his cup contained red wine and not coffee.

Now, General Patton could never, never be wrong. Without hesitating he replied, "I know. I like my wine this way." And he drank it!

I relate this story because I see something of myself, and perhaps most of us, here. It is difficult to admit mistakes. It is hard to admit when we are wrong.

Three of life's most difficult words to say are, "I was wrong." But they are also three of the most powerful words we can utter. "I was wrong" breaks down barriers between people. It brings estranged people together. And it creates a climate where intimacy and love may flourish. You may be surprised at how positively many people respond to the words, "I was wrong"!

Naturally, it is a risk. But to admit when you are wrong is not to confess that you are a "bad" person. Simply an honest one. And true friends will appreciate you for it.

Whole and happy lives are built by people who have learned the power of intimacy, in part, through the use of the words "I was wrong."

Ten Other Commandments

1. You shall not worry, for worry is the most unproductive of all human activities.

2. You shall not be fearful, for most of the things you fear will never come to pass.

3. You shall not carry grudges, for they are the heaviest of all life's burdens.

4. You shall face each problem as it comes. You can only handle one at a time anyway.

5. You shall not take problems to bed with you, for they make very poor bedfellows.

6. You shall not borrow other people's problems. They can better care for them than you.

7. You shall not try to relive yesterday for good or ill, it is forever gone. Concentrate on what is happening in your life and be happy now!

8. You shall be a good listener, for only when you listen do you hear ideas different from your own.

9. You shall not become "bogged down" by frustration, for 90% of it is rooted in self-pity and will only interfere with positive action.

10. You shall count your blessings, never overlooking the small ones, for a lot of small blessings add up to a big one.

(Author unknown)

P.S.

Another piece of advice we heard along the way -- never buy a Rolex from someone who is out of breath...

Losing the Dead Part

I am discovering that many people want, above all else, to live life fully. But sometimes the past prohibits our living and enjoying life to the utmost in the present.

A school teacher entered his room a few minutes early and noticed a meal worm laboriously crawling along the floor. It had somehow been injured. The back part of the worm was dead and dried up, but still attached to the front, living part by just a thin thread.

As the teacher studied the strange sight of a poor worm pulling its dead half across the floor, a little girl ran in and noticed it there. Picking it up, she said, "Oh, Oscar, when are you going to lose that dead part so you can really live?"

What a marvelous question for all of us! When are we going to lose that dead part so we can really live? When are we going to let go of past pain so we can live fully? When are we going to drop the baggage of needless guilt so we can experience life? When are we going to let go of that past resentment so we can know peace?

Have you been dragging something that is dead and gone around with you? Are you ready to "lose that dead part so you can really live"?

A Cure For Loneliness

People do strange things! I heard of a man who occasionally swallowed coins -- enough to make him sick! Which, as it turns out, was the whole idea. When asked why he made himself sick swallowing coins, he replied that he enjoyed the affection and attention which the staff showed him in the hospital!

He was lonely. Many of us are lonely. When asked, "What is life's heaviest burden?" one lonely old man answered, "To have nothing to carry."

A cure for loneliness is to carry the burden of another. Get involved with their problems. Visit others who are also lonely. Listen to someone else's troubles. Find people who need you and do something for them. Carrying another's burden will lighten the load of your loneliness.

I know a woman who gave each person in her family a golden angel lapel pin one Christmas. "Wear it on your collar or shoulder," she said, "to remind you that your guardian angel is always looking over your shoulder."

Her brother noticed his pin had a broken wing. He held up his damaged angel and quipped, "It figures. *My* guardian angel is missing a wing. She can't even take care of herself!"

Two years later he died of cancer. As I thought of the pain his family must be feeling, I was struck with how his broken angel is like each of us. We each hurt. We all experience loss. At times we are lonely. Like that angel, we are each broken in some way, even if our damage is interior and invisible to others.

But we're each like his broken angel in another way, too. As it has been so beautifully said, "We are all like angels with just one wing. We can only fly by embracing each other." You see, we will heal best by hanging on to one another. And we will overcome loneliness best by putting an arm around someone else and going it with them.

This family embraced each other. And as they carried one another's burdens, their own loads were lightened. It's a solution for loneliness -- and a formula for happiness.

P.S.

Jules Renard says, "Love is like an hour-glass, with the heart filling up as the brain empties."

A Peculiar Kind of Love

It was love at first sight. I knew how the boy felt who clambered breathlessly through his front door and cried, "Dad! I'm in love!"

"How do you know it's love?" his father asked.

"Because, when I kissed her good-night, her dog bit me and I never even felt it 'til I got home!"

I can relate to him, because even without the dog-bite test, I knew love when it bit me. And it must have bit her, too, because a few weeks later she asked me to marry her! Before long, though, I began to notice something "peculiar" about her love. She sometimes said, "I love you too much to hold on to you." And she said, "I want you to be happy... even if that means we won't be together."

Another time she said, "I love you so much I want to let you go. Don't feel tied to me."

Talk like that sounded peculiar to me. You see, my love was a little different. "I love you so much I want to always keep you with me," better described my kind of love. "I love you too much to ever let you go," was more typical of how I felt.

My love was a hanging-on kind of love. Hers was a letting-go kind of love. My love worried about what it might do to me if I lost her. Her love worried about what it might do to us if she hung on too tightly.

One day she returned from a doctor's appointment distraught. "He told me I can't have babies," she said. Her swollen eyes overflowed. "I know you want children. I'll understand if you don't want to marry," she continued. "I love you too much to keep you." There again -- that peculiar letting-go kind of love.

All of this happened many years ago and, in the meantime, I have learned something about love. Love can sometimes be about hanging on. But it can also be about letting go. It is as simple and as difficult as that.

And I learned something else, too. The doctor was wrong about the babies!

How about you? Is your love one of hanging on, or of letting go?

Retaliate in Kindness

I heard about a woman who sued her husband for divorce. She told the judge she had nagged and nagged, but she couldn't get him to do right.

The judge wondered if she had tried using kindness. Referring to the biblical passage which says that when we show kindness to our enemy it is like heaping "burning coals on his head," he asked her if she had tried heaping coals on his head.

She answered, "No, but I don't think it will work. I already tried scalding water and that didn't do any good." (Ouch...)

Who hasn't felt frustrated with another? Who hasn't wanted to strike out rather than reach out? But revenge is never as sweet as we imagine it to be. And besides, when we fight fire with fire, everybody is likely to get burned.

Next time you get upset try this: retaliate in kindness, not in kind. Turn your anger into an assault of good will! After all, who can resist a barrage of kindness?

P.S.

Kindness is difficult to give away 'cause it keeps coming back.

Taking Chances, Making Chances

Lecturer Charles Hobbs sometimes tells about a woman who lived in London over a century ago. She saved what little money she could working as a scullery maid and used it one evening to hear a great speaker of her day. His speech moved her deeply and she waited to visit with him afterward. "How fine it must be to have had the opportunities you have had in life," she said.

"My dear lady," he replied, "have you never received an opportunity?"

"Not me. I have never had a chance," she said.

"What do you do?" the speaker asked.

She answered, "I peel onions and potatoes in my sister's boarding house."

"How long have you been doing this?" he pursued.

"Fifteen miserable years!"

"And where do you sit?" he continued.

"Why, on the bottom step in the kitchen." She looked puzzled.

"And where do you put your feet?"

"On the floor," she answered, more puzzled.

"What is the floor?"

"It is glazed brick."

Then he said, "My dear lady, I will give you an assignment today. I want you to write me a letter about the brick."

Against her protests about being a poor writer, he made her promise to complete the assignment.

The next day, as she sat down to peel onions, she gazed at the brick floor. That evening she pulled one loose, took it to a brick factory and asked the owner to explain to her how bricks were made.

Still not satisfied, she went to a library and found a book on bricks. She learned that 120 different kinds of brick and tile were being produced in England at the time. She discovered how clay beds, which existed for millions of years, were formed. Her research captivated her imagination and she spent every spare moment learning more. She returned to the library night after night and this woman, who never had a chance, gradually began to climb the steps of knowledge.

After months of study, she set out to write her letter as promised. She sent a 36-page document about the brick in her kitchen and, to her surprise, she received a letter back. Enclosed was payment for her research. He had published her letter! And along with the money came a new assignment -- this time he asked her to write about what she found *underneath* the brick.

For the first time in her life she could hardly wait to get back to the kitchen! She pulled up the brick and there was an ant. She held it in her hand and examined it.

That evening, she hurried back to the library to study ants. She learned that there were hundreds of different kinds of ants. Some were so small they could stand on the head of a pin, while others were so large one could feel the weight of them in one's hand. She started her own ant colony and examined ants underneath a lens.

Several months later she wrote her findings in a 350-page "letter." It, too, was eventually published. She soon quit her kitchen job to take up writing.

Before she died, she had traveled to the lands of her dreams and had experienced more than she ever imagined possible! This is the woman who had never had a chance.

Some people wait for opportunity to come knocking. Here is a person who sought it out, proving again that we can be more than victims of mere circumstance.

If given a chance, will you take it? If given no chance, can you make one?

The Gadget That Gets Me Started

A funny story has it that, late one night, a party-goer decided it would be best to walk home. He found a short cut through a poorly-lit cemetery and, in the darkness, stumbled into an open grave.

He tried to climb out but the walls were too slippery. Again and again he fell back into the grave. Finally, in exhaustion, he settled in a corner to wait for sunlight.

A few minutes later another man cutting through the cemetery fell victim to the same grave. He, too, tried desperately to climb and claw his way out, and he was equally unsuccessful.

As he was about to give up in hopeless resignation, he heard a voice from the darkness of his pit: "You'll never get out of here." He did!

He just needed the proper motivation. And in this case, a shot of fear did the trick. But when it comes to finding the motivation to accomplish most worthwhile things, his example is the exception.

I am learning that the best motivation, whether we want to accomplish a task, go back to school, start something new or kick a habit, usually comes from the inside. To be successful, we must *want* to do it. Others may certainly help to encourage or to "pump us up," but, in the end, we will usually succeed only if we have the desire.

Dorothy Heller illustrates this with an all-too-true poem:

> *I spent a fortune*
> *On a trampoline,*
> *A stationary bike*
> *And a rowing machine*
> *Complete with gadgets*
> *To read my pulse,*
> *And gadgets to prove*
> *My progress results,*
> *And others to show*
> *The miles I've charted --*
> *But they left off the gadget*
> *To get me started!*

Of course they left it off! The gadget to get us started lies within!

P.S.

Bill Cosby says, "I don't know the key to success, but the key to failure is trying to please everybody."

What Children Want

Are you aware of the first Law of Parenthood? It states that nobody really wants your job, but everybody thinks they can do it better.

I appreciate the honesty of parents who sometimes feel overwhelmed by the task of parenthood. One man candidly said, "Before I got married I had three theories on raising children. Now I have three children and no theories!"

Quote Magazine (September 1, 1985) published ten behaviors children ages 8 to 14 identified as qualities they wanted in parents. These young people, from 24 countries, agreed on 10 traits they believed were important for all parents to possess. Here they are:

1. They want harmony. They do not want their parents to have unresolved and destructive conflict in front of them.

2. They want love. They wish to be treated with the same affection as other children in the family.

3. They want honesty. And to be told the truth.

4. They want acceptance. They desire mutual tolerance from both parents.

5. They want their parents to like their friends. They want their friends to be welcomed in the home.

6. They want closeness. They desire comradeship with their parents.

7. They want their parents to pay attention to them and answer their questions.

8. They want consideration from their parents. They do not want to be embarrassed or punished in front of friends.

9. They want positive support. They wish for their parents to concentrate on their good points rather than their weaknesses.

10. They want consistency. They desire parents to be constant in their affections and moods.

It appears that these children want what all of us want -- respect, consideration and love. In fact, these work well with "children" of *all* ages!

Wait Training

Perhaps you can relate. One man was to meet his wife downtown and spend some time shopping with her. He waited patiently for 15 minutes. Then he waited impatiently for 15 minutes more.

After that, he became angry. Seeing one of those photograph booths nearby (the kind that accepts coins into a slot and takes four shots while you pose on a small bench), he had an idea. He assumed the most ferocious expression he could manage, which wasn't difficult under the circumstances, and in a few moments he was holding four small prints that shocked even him!

He wrote his wife's name on the back of the photographs and handed them to a clerk behind the desk. "If you see a small, dark lady with brown eyes and an apologetic expression, apparently looking for someone, would you please give her this?" he said.

He then returned to his office content that, if a picture is worth a thousand words, then four photos must be a full-blown lecture!

His wife saved those pictures. She carries them in her purse now. Shows them to anyone who asks if she is married...

How are you with patience? One person calls it "wait-training." It seems that there is always something we are waiting for. We wait on traffic and we wait in lines. We wait to hear about a new job. We wait to complete school or to retire. We wait to grow up or for maturity in a child. We wait for a decision to be made. We wait for someone to change his or her mind.

Patience is an essential quality of a happy life. After all, some things are worth waiting for. Every day presents plenty of opportunities for wait-training.

We can resent waiting, accept it or even get good at it! But one thing is certain -- we cannot avoid it. How is your wait-training coming along?

P.S.

Speaking of patience, it isn't fair -- there should be a better reward for promptness than having to wait for everyone else!

Pecking Away

Do you know when to give up and when to keep trying? Former University of Alabama president, Frank Rose, used to tell a favorite story about a time, in the mid-1960s, when evangelist Billy Graham was invited to speak at an event in the university's football stadium. There were 18,000 people in attendance that evening. America's civil rights movement was well underway and the stadium crowd represented one of the largest racially integrated meetings ever held in the state.

As Rev. Graham was giving a message about easing racial tensions, a huge thunderstorm gathered overhead. Suddenly, lightening struck and a ball of fire seemed to emanate from the speaker's microphone and travel down the wire.

Graham immediately sat down. Then he leaned over and spoke to Alabama's legendary football coach, Bear Bryant. "Coach," he said, "you'd have stopped, too, if that lightnin' had hit you like that."

Bear said, "No sir!"

"What do you mean?" asked Graham.

"Well," he said, "if I was down on the one-yard line, I wouldn't have stopped until I scored."

At that, Rev. Graham returned to the microphone and finished his talk.

Safety considerations aside, the story reminds us of one of life's important lessons. In most of what we do, there is a time to stop, but there is also a time to score; a time to pack it in, but also a time to complete the task. The woodpecker owes its success to the fact that it uses it's head and keeps pecking away until it finishes the job!

Today, will you quit? Or will you keep pecking away?

Contentment Now

Are you waiting for "things to calm down" a bit before you can be at peace? Inner peace eludes many people who expect to discover it after things calm down, slow down or finally run down. But some wisdom from antiquity, attributed to Montaigne, tells a different story about inner peace.

He tells that when King Pyrrhus prepared for his expedition into Italy, his wise counselor Cyness drew him aside and implored him to reconsider his aggressive activity. "Sir," he asked the king, "to what end do you make all this mighty preparation?"

"To make myself master of Italy," replied King Pyrrhus.

"And what after that is done?" asked his counselor.

"I will pass into Gaul and Spain."

"And what then?"

"I will then go to subdue Africa; and lastly, when I have brought the whole world to my subjection, I will sit down and rest content at my own ease."

"For God's sake, sir," replied Cyness. "Tell me what hinders that you may not, if you please, be now in the condition you speak of? Why do you not now at this instant, settle yourself in the state you seem to aim at, and spare all the labor and hazard you interpose?"

Gratefully, we are learning different attitudes today about war and peace. But can Cyness' advice apply to our hectic and conflicted lives?

What keeps you from the inner peace and contentment you crave now? Must life's battles be fought and won before you can be satisfied? Or can you, at this instant, settle yourself in a state of quiet even though all around you is not under your control?

P.S.

P.S. Ever felt like the harried parent who announced, "One day I shall burst my buds of calm and blossom into hysteria..."? Poetic, actually.

My Reality is Virtual!

Someone once quipped, "A lot of my reality is virtual!" Whether or not you can say the same thing, I find it is true that a lot of my reality is the way I perceive it. Let me explain what I mean with a true story.

In the "Journal of the American Medical Association," Dr. Paul Ruskin demonstrated how our perception of reality (not actually what is going on, but how we perceive it) determines how we feel about it. While teaching a class on the psychological aspects of aging, he read the following case to his students:

The patient neither speaks nor comprehends the spoken word. Sometimes she babbles incoherently for hours on end. She is disoriented about person, place, and time. She does, however, respond to her name. I have worked with her for the past six months, but she still shows complete disregard for her physical appearance and makes no effort to assist her own care. She must be fed, bathed, and clothed by others. Because she has no teeth, her food must be pureed. Her shirt is usually soiled from almost incessant drooling. She does not walk. Her sleep pattern is erratic. Often she wakes in the middle of the night, and her screaming awakens others. Most of the time she is friendly and happy, but several times a day she gets quite agitated without apparent cause. Then she wails until someone comes to comfort her.

After presenting the case, Dr. Ruskin asked his students how they would like caring for this person. Most of them said they would not like it at all. He then said that he believed he would especially enjoy it, and thought that they might, also. He passed a picture of the patient around for his puzzled students to see. It was his six-month-old daughter!

Most of the students had already made up their minds that they would not like caring for such a patient. But the age of the patient, rather than the actual duties, made the task seem fun and enjoyable! When they thought the task might be fun, they were positive about it, though their reaction just moments before was quite negative.

You and I have numerous tasks ahead. How will you look at them today? As pleasant or unpleasant? As chores or as fun? When you think you may actually *enjoy* them -- you probably will!

The Most Difficult Instrument to Play

Do you know what is the hardest instrument in the orchestra to play? The hardest instrument to play is second fiddle. While all the rest of the instruments have their own sections, the violins are divided into two parts -- "first" and "second" violins.

First violins are often the stars of the show. They get the melody lines. They get to show off. They sit next to the audience.

Back behind, where they are hard to see, are the second violins. They play a supporting role. They play harmony to the first violins. Theirs is a service role. Their job is to round out the sound of the other instruments. They serve the orchestra. They do what is not glamorous so that the whole will be beautiful. Without the second violins, the orchestra would sound incomplete.

You know what the hardest role to play in life is? Second fiddle. To play second fiddle is to play a supporting role for someone else. And it is sometimes a service role; doing what is not glamorous, usually behind the scenes, so that the whole can be more beautiful.

The late Leo Buscaglia, that effervescent educator, speaker, author, and lover of life, used to tell his university students that there is a world out there dying to be loved! He challenged his students to love and often told them that serving others is the way they can find such things as happiness and joy.

He sometimes told about Joel. Leo got Joel hooked on serving. He took him to a nursing home and said, "You see that woman sitting over there? I want you to go and introduce yourself to her."

Joel was not looking forward to his nursing home visit. But he nevertheless went to the stranger and introduced himself. She looked at him skeptically and asked, "Are you one of my relatives?"

Joel answered, "No. I'm not."

And she said, "Good, I hate my relatives. Sit down, son, and talk to me." He did and they talked.

He went back the next week. And the next. They developed a close friendship and Joel soon looked forward to his visits. He learned something about the joy of serving. About working behind the scenes. About playing second fiddle. And he made one woman's world a little more beautiful.

P.S.

"If you ever need a helping hand, you'll find one at the end of your arm. As you grow older, you will discover that you have two hands. One for helping yourself, the other for helping others."

Riches of the Heart

A funny story is told about a young woman who confided to her new lover, "My father is gone and my mother is in very poor health. It looks as if she will die soon and I will inherit all her money. We should get married; after all I'm going to be a millionaire!" Two weeks later the man became her stepfather.

I have heard it said that from the time an infant first struggles to get her toes into her mouth, life is a continual struggle to make both ends meet. Those who are working one or more jobs and feel as if they are barely getting by, can relate.

But I also know that the pursuit of money, as an end in itself, is an empty endeavor. Happy are those who seek riches which cannot be counted in a bank or measured on a scale. For they will never know real poverty.

I believe writer Rudyard Kipling got it right when he admonished students at McGill University to never waste their time fighting for money. He said that some day they will meet someone who cares little for money and will not take it, even if offered. At that time, they will discover how poor they really are!

Yet how very wealthy are those who seek riches of the heart. They will always have more than enough of all that brings true happiness.

Index

Index, cont.

Quick Order Form

☞ **F**ax Orders: (413) 431-3499 Send this form.

☞ **T**elephone Orders: Toll free (877) 344-0989
Please have your credit card ready.

☞ **W**eb Site Orders: visit
http://www.LifeSupportSystem.com/books

☞ **P**ostal Orders: Life Support System Publishing, Inc.
P. O. Box 260804, Highlands Ranch, CO 80163-0804
USA

Order these books by Steve Goodier ($12.95 US)

❑ *One Minute Can Change a Life*   Quantity_____
❑ *Riches of the Heart*   Quantity_____

Name_____

Address_____

_____

FREE Shipping and Handling for U.S.A. Orders
Canada: $2.00 / order   Other International: $4.00 / order

Payment: ___ Check ___ Credit Card:
___Visa ___Master Card ___AMEX

Card no: _____Exp. date: _____

Name on Card: _____

Receive daily inspirational e-mail FREE... visit:
www.LifeSupportSystem.com

Quick Order Form

☞ Fax Orders: (413) 431-3499 Send this form.

☞ Telephone Orders: Toll free (877) 344-0989
Please have your credit card ready.

☞ Web Site Orders: visit
http://www.LifeSupportSystem.com/books

☞ Postal Orders: Life Support System Publishing, Inc.
P. O. Box 260804, Highlands Ranch, CO 80163-0804
USA

Order these books by Steve Goodier ($12.95 US)

❑ *One Minute Can Change a Life*   Quantity_____
❑ *Riches of the Heart*   Quantity_____

Name_____

Address_____

_____

FREE Shipping and Handling for U.S.A. Orders
Canada: $2.00 / order   Other International: $4.00 / order

Payment: ___ Check   ___ Credit Card:
___Visa ___Master Card ___AMEX

Card no: _____Exp. date: _____

Name on Card: _____

Receive daily inspirational e-mail FREE... visit:
www.LifeSupportSystem.com